AMARILLO SKY

Words and Music by
JOHN RICH, KENNY ALPHIN,
RODNEY CLAWSON and BART PURSLEY

Amarillo Sky - 5 - 1

2007

PIANO · VOCAL · CHORDS

COUNTRY SUPERSTARS
SHEET MUSIC

 PlayList

SONGS THAT MADE THE YEAR!

Alfred Publishing Co., Inc.
16320 Roscoe Blvd., Suite 100
P.O. Box 10003
Van Nuys, CA 91410-0003
alfred.com

ISBN-10: 0-7390-5039-7
ISBN-13: 978-0-7390-5039-2

CONTENTS

SONG	TITLE	PAGE
Amarillo Sky	Jason Aldean	3
Anyway	Martina McBride	8
As If	Sara Evans	14
Because of You	Reba McEntire and Kelly Clarkson	20
Bring It on Home	Little Big Town	26
Don't Blink	Kenny Chesney	32
How I Feel	Martina McBride	37
How Long	Eagles	43
If You're Reading This	Tim McGraw	57
I'll Stand by You	Carrie Underwood	51
Johnny Cash	Jason Aldean	63
Leave the Pieces	The Wreckers	69
A Little More You	Little Big Town	74
Lost	Faith Hill	81
Lost in This Moment	Big & Rich	88
Moments	Emerson Drive	93
More	Rockie Lynn	99
More Than a Memory	Garth Brooks	104
Not Ready to Make Nice	Dixie Chicks	111
Nothin' Better to Do	LeAnn Rimes	118
Proud of the House We Built	Brooks & Dunn	125
The Reason Why	Vince Gill	132
So Small	Carrie Underwood	135
Some People Change	Montgomery Gentry	143
Stupid Boy	Keith Urban	149
Take Me There	Rascal Flatts	159
Tough	Craig Morgan	166
Wasted	Carrie Underwood	171
Watching You	Rodney Atkins	176
Way Back Texas	Pat Green	182
Whenever You Remember	Carrie Underwood	189
A Woman's Love	Alan Jackson	194
You Never Take Me Dancing	Travis Tritt	199

6

Chorus:

takes the trac - tor an - oth - er round, an - oth - er round,_ an - oth - er round. And he

takes the trac - tor an - oth - er round, an - oth - er round,_____ and says, "I

nev - er com - plain, I nev - er ask why. Please don't let my dreams_ a - run dry_____

ANYWAY

Words and Music by
MARTINA McBRIDE, BRAD WARREN
and BRETT WARREN

Anyway - 6 - 1

AS IF

Words and Music by
JOHN SHANKS, SARA EVANS
and HILARY LINDSEY

18

Chorus:

worn - out blue jeans, walk - ing all a - round_ in the big sun -

shine._____ 'Cause I'm
(I,   I'm._____)

act - ing as___ if this___ blue sky's nev - er gon - na rain down_ on me._

I'm
(I,   I'm._____)
tell - ing my - self this___ true love's nev - er gon - na

BECAUSE OF YOU

Words and Music by
KELLY CLARKSON, BEN MOODY
and DAVID HODGES

Slowly ♩ = 69

Verse 1 (sing 1st time only):

Reba:

1. I will___ not make the same___

Verse 2 (sing 2nd time only):

Kelly:

2. I lose___ my way and it's

___ mis-takes___ that you___ did. I will___ not let my-self

not too long___ be-fore___ you point it out. I can-not cry, be-

BRING IT ON HOME

Words and Music by
WAYNE KIRKPATRICK, GREG BIECK
and TYLER HAYES-BIECK

But don't you keep__ it to__ your - self._____ When your long_

𝄋 Chorus:

day__ is o - ver, and you can bare-

ly drag__ your____ feet, the weight of the

world_____ is on__ your shoul - ders, I know what you need,-

To Coda ⊕

*Vocal harmonies are written at pitch.

to me.___ You got some - one here who wants to make it al - right, some-

one that loves___ you more___ than life___ right_____ here.___

molto rit.

Verse 2:
You know I know you like the back of my hand.
Did you know I'm gonna do all that I can right here?
I'm gonna lie with you till you fall asleep.
When the morning comes, I'm still gonna be right here.
Take your worries and just drop them at the door.
Baby, leave it all behind.
(To Chorus:)

DON'T BLINK

Words and Music by
CHRIS WALLIN and CASEY BEATHARD

Moderately slow ♩ = 76

1. I turned on the eve-ning news, saw an old man be-ing in-ter-viewed,___
2. I was glued to my___ T V, when it looked like he looked at me and said,

turn-ing a hun-dred and two___ to-day.
"Best start put-tin' first___ things first.
'Cause when your

They asked him, "What's the se-cret to life?"___
hour-glass runs out of sand,___ you can't
He looked up___ from his___ old pipe,___
flip it o-ver and start a-gain.___

Don't Blink - 5 - 1

Chorus:

laughed, and said,___ "All I___ can say___ is:
Take ev-'ry breath God gives you for what it's worth.___ } Don't___

blink.___ Just___ like that,___ you're six___ years old___ and you're tak-in' naps, and you

wake up___ and you're twen-ty-five,___ and your high___ school sweet-heart be-comes your wife. Don't___

___ blink.___ You just___ might miss___ your ba-bies grow-in' like___ mine did,___

34

Don't Blink - 5 - 3

HOW I FEEL

Words and Music by
MARTINA McBRIDE, BRAD WARREN,
BRETT WARREN, CHRIS LINDSEY
and AIMEE MAYO

Moderately slow ($\quarternote$ = 104)

Verse:

fet-ti fall-in'_____ the first from the sky;_____

luck-y coat,_____ the first day of fall,_____

How I Feel - 6 - 1

when you wake up laugh-ing

my home - town___

on the Fourth of Ju - ly;___

just___ be - cause.___

An old church

___ a mid-night snow___ on Christ-

door___ that stays___

mas Eve;___ like stand-in' up___ for what___ you be - lieve.___ That's

___ wide___ o - pen, a per - fect heart___ that's nev - er been bro - ken. That's

cresc.

Chorus 1 & 2:

how I feel___ when I'm___ with___ you.___ That's how I feel___ when___ I'm___

mf

Chorus 3:

when I'm___ with you.___

HOW LONG

Words and Music by
J. D. SOUTHER

Moderately fast ♩ = 138

Verse 1:

1. Like a blue - bird_____ with his heart_____ re - moved,_____ lone - ly as a train,_____ I've run just as far_____

I'LL STAND BY YOU

Words and Music by
BILLY STEINBERG, TOM KELLY
and CHRISSIE HYNDE

Verse 1:

1. Oh, why you look so sad? The tears are in your eyes. Come on and come to me now. Don't be a-shamed to cry, let me see you

I'll Stand by You - 6 - 1

IF YOU'RE READING THIS

Words and Music by
TIM McGRAW, BRAD WARREN
and BRETT WARREN

60

reading this, I'm already home.

2. If you're reading this, I'm already home.

3. If you're

Verse 3:

reading this, there's gonna come a day when

read-ing this, if you're read-ing this, I'm al - read-y home.

Verse 2:
If you're reading this, halfway around the world,
I won't be there to see the birth of our little girl.
I hope she looks like you, I hope she fights like me,
And stands up for the innocent and the weak.
I'm laying down my gun, I'm hanging up my boots.
Tell Dad I don't regret that I followed in his shoes.
(To Chorus:)

JOHNNY CASH

Words and Music by
VICKY McGEHEE, RODNEY CLAWSON
and JOHN RICH

Gtr. tuned down 1/2 step:
⑥ = E♭   ③ = G♭
⑤ = A♭   ② = B♭
④ = D♭   ① = E♭

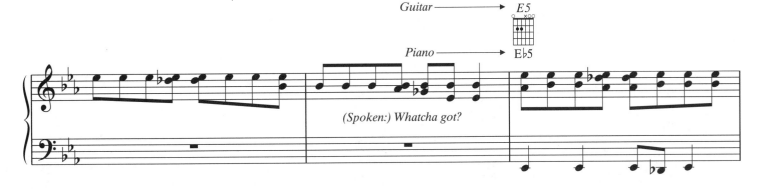

(Spoken:) Whatcha got?

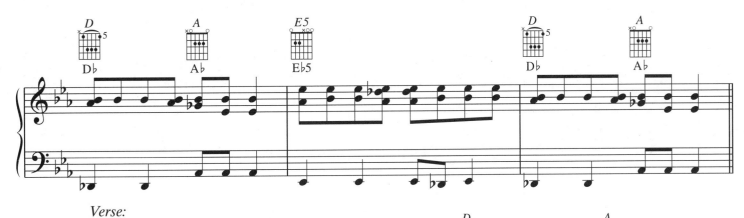

Verse:

1. Quit__ my   job,   flipped off the boss,   took my name off the pay-
2. It's four hun-dred and six-ty-sev-en   miles__   to the out-skirts   of Las

Johnny Cash - 6 - 1

64

Wait out by the road;___ I'm com-in' to pick___ you up."___
send her a sou - ve - nir post - card from the wild side.___

𝄋 *Chorus:*

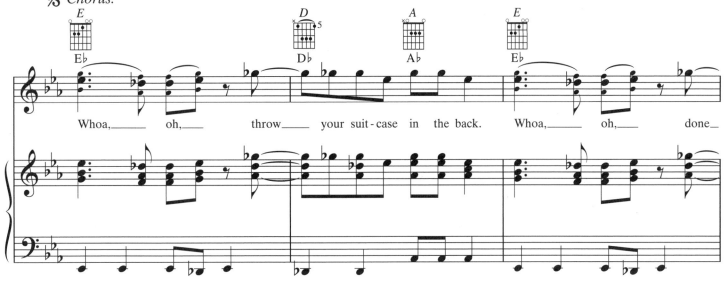

Whoa,___ oh,___ throw___ your suit - case in the back. Whoa,___ oh,___ done___

___ gassed up the Pon - ti - ac. Whoa,___ oh,___ blast - in' out to John - ny Cash.

LEAVE THE PIECES

Words and Music by
BILLY AUSTIN and JENNIFER HANSON

1. Well, you're not sure that you love me, but you're not
drag out the heart-ache,

sure e-nough to let me go. Ba-by, it ain't fair, you know, to just
ba-by, you can make it quick. Real-ly, get it o-ver with and just

*Original recording in D♭ major with guitar tuned down a half step

Leave the Pieces - 5 - 1

71

Leave the Pieces - 5 - 3

A LITTLE MORE YOU

Words and Music by
WAYNE KIRKPATRICK, JIMI WESTBROOK,
KAREN CHILDERS, KIMBERLY ROADS
and PHILLIP SWEET

A Little More You - 7 - 1

Verse 3:
You're teasin' me with a touch and the whole world shakes.
Keep holdin' that river back and the levee may break.
There's only so much that this ol' boy can take.
Come on, baby, give me a little more you.
Come on, baby, give me a little more you.
(To Chorus:)

LOST

Words and Music by
KARA DIOGUARDI and MITCH ALLAN

being lost means that I'm nev-er gon-na be with-out____ you, I wan-na stay lost for-ev-

decresc.

er.____ I wan-na stay lost for-ev-

mp

er____ with you.

rit.

LOST IN THIS MOMENT

Words and Music by
JOHN D. RICH, RODNEY CLAWSON
and KEITH ANDERSON

Verse 1:

1. I see your ma-ma and the can-dles and the tears and ro - ses.

I see your dad-dy walk his daugh-ter down the aisle.

And my knees start to trem-ble as I tell the preach-er,__ "Don't she look__ beau-ti - ful_____

Repeat ad lib. and fade

my dreams come true,___ lost in this mo - ment with you.___ Lost in the mo-

ment,_____ in___ this mo - ment with you.___ Lost in the mo-

ment, yeah._____ Ooh,___ lost in the mo-

Verse 3:
I smell the jasmine floating in the air like a love song,
Watch my words draw sweet tears from your eyes.
Bow our heads while the preacher talks to Jesus,
Please bless this brand-new life, yeah.
(To Chorus:)

MOMENTS

Words and Music by
DAVE BERG, SAM TATE
and ANNIE TATE

Moments - 6 - 1

I've had my mo - ments.

I've had my mo - ments.

Repeat ad lib. and fade

MORE

Words and Music by
DENNIS MORGAN and ROCKIE LYNNE

Moderately slow (♩ = 100)

(with pedal)

Verse:

1. You say I am__ your ev - 'ry - thing,__ the half__ that makes__ you whole.__ You

2. *See additional lyrics*

say you love__ me with all___ your heart,__ your bod - y and__ your soul.__ You

say your love__ is an o - cean with-out an - y shore.__ You

More - 5 - 1

Verse 2:
Waking up with you in the morning
And seeing your smiling face
Makes me feel like God
Has put us in a permanent state of grace.
Your kiss tells me you need me
Like nobody has before.
You say how much you want me,
But I want you more...
(To Bridge:)

MORE THAN A MEMORY

Words and Music by
BILLY MONTANA, LEE BRICE
and KYLE JACOBS

More Than a Memory - 7 - 1

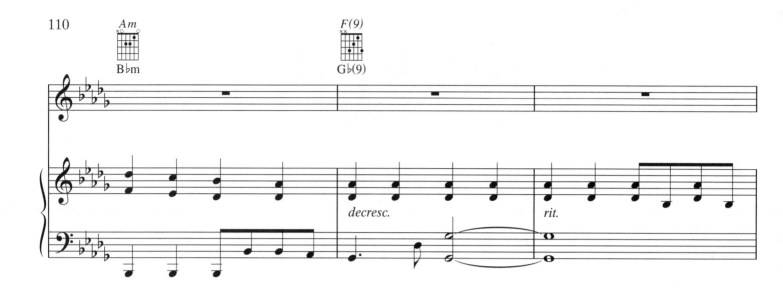

A little slower ♩ = 63

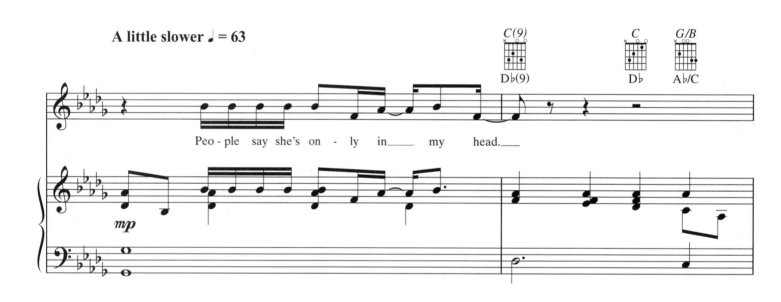

Peo - ple say she's on - ly in____ my head.___

mp

It's gon - na take time, but I'll____ *for - get.*

rit.

NOT READY TO MAKE NICE

Words and Music by
EMILY ROBISON, MARTIE MAGUIRE,
NATALIE MAINES and DAN WILSON

*Original recording in F# major with guitar tuned down a half step.

Not Ready to Make Nice - 7 - 1

114

Chorus:

NOTHIN' BETTER TO DO

Words and Music by
LEANN RIMES, DEAN SHEREMET
and DARRELL BROWN

Moderately ♩ = 92

Guitar Capo 1 →

Piano →

Verse:

1. Hung _____ my cot-ton dress on rust-ed wire,
2. Sign _____ read, "Bait, chips, beer and am-mu-ni-

tion." _____
up there on Pe-la-hat-chie Bridge.
That Slim-Jim bag boy had-n't a prayer.

Nothin' Better to Do - 7 - 1

Yeah.

(Inst. solo ad lib....

...end solo)

Bridge:

No - bod - y hurt,___ no - bod - y harmed,___ no - bod - y's bus - 'ness but___ my

own._____ Ma - ma said, "I - dle hands_ are dev - il's hand - i - work."_ Oh,

the trou - ble you'll get in - to._____ You_ got

Chorus:

noth - in' bet - ter to do,___ got noth - in' bet - ter to do.___ You_ got

noth - in' bet - ter to do,___ got noth - in' bet - ter to do.___ You got___

Nothin' Better to Do - 7 - 6

PROUD OF THE HOUSE WE BUILT

Words and Music by
MARV GREEN, RONNIE DUNN
and TERRY McBRIDE

130

Chorus:

THE REASON WHY

Words and Music by
VINCE GILL and GARY NICHOLSON

* Sing harmony 2nd time only.

The Reason Why - 3 - 1

Verse 3:

SO SMALL

Words and Music by
CARRIE UNDERWOOD, HILLARY LINDSEY
and LUKE LAIRD

Slowly ♩ = 76

Guitar Capo 1
Piano

Bm7 / Cm7 *G(9) / A♭(9)* *D / E♭* *A / B♭*

(with pedal)

Yeah,___

yeah.___

Verse 1:

Bm / Cm *G / A♭* *D / E♭* *A / B♭*

1. What you got if you ain't___ got love, the kind that___ you just___ want to give a - way?___

SOME PEOPLE CHANGE

Words and Music by
NEIL THRASHER, MICHAEL DULANEY
and JASON SELLERS

Moderately slow country rock ♩ = 84

Verse 1:

1. His old man was a reb-el yel-ler, bad boy to the bone,___ he'd say. Can't trust that___ oth-er fel-ler. He'd judge 'em by the tone___ of their skin.___

Some People Change - 6 - 1

148

*Sing first time only.

STUPID BOY

Gtr. tuned down 1/2 step:
⑥ = E♭   ③ = G♭
⑤ = A♭   ② = B♭
④ = D♭   ① = E♭

Words and Music by
DEANNA BRYANT, DAVE BERG
and SARAH BUXTON

Moderately slow ♩ = 76

Verse 1:

1. Well, she was pre-cious, like a flow-er.   She grew wild,_

Stupid Boy - 10 - 1

Stupid Boy - 10 - 3

156 *Verse 3:*

3. It took a while___ for her to fig-ure out   she could run,   but when she did,

she was___   long gone,_ long___   gone.___

a tempo

TAKE ME THERE

Words and Music by
WENDELL MOBLEY, NEIL THRASHER
and KENNY CHESNEY

Moderately slow ♩ = 92

Take Me There - 7 - 1

Chorus:

I_____ wan-na know ev-'ry-thing_____ a-

bout you_____ then. And

I_____ wan-na go down ev-'ry

road you've_____ been. Where your

TOUGH

Words and Music by
JOE LEATHERS and MONTY CRISWELL

Tough - 5 - 1

Chorus:

strong, push-es on; can't____ slow her down._____ She can

take an-y-thing life____ dish-es out.____ There

was a time,___ back___ be-fore she was mine,_____ when I thought I____ was tough.

WASTED

Words and Music by
MARV GREEN, TROY VERGES
and HILLARY LINDSEY

Moderately ♩ = 92

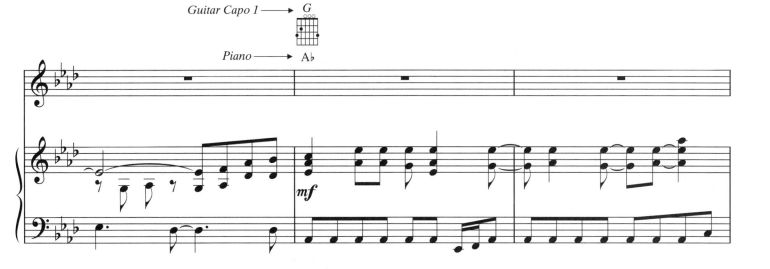

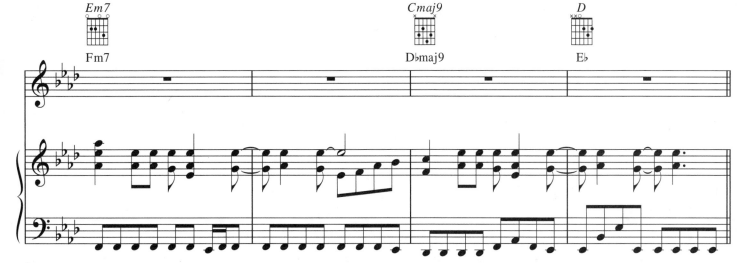

Wasted - 5 - 1

%S *Verse:*

1. Stand - ing at___ the back___ door, she tried to make___ it fast.___
2.3. *See additional lyrics*

One tear hit the hard - wood; it fell___ like bro - ken glass.___ She said, "Some -

times love slips a - way___ and you just___ can't get it back, let's face___

___ it." 2. For

Chorus:

1. 2. I don't wan - na spend my life jad - ed, wait - in', to
(3.) I don't wan - na keep on wish - in', miss - in' the

wake up one day___ and find_____ that I let___
still of the morn - in', the col - or of the night.___ I ain't spend-

___ all these years___ go by,___ wast - ed.___
in' no___ more time___ wast - ed.___

1.   *D.S.* % 2.   3.

3. An -   3. Oh,_____

Bridge:

She kept driv - in' a - long____ 'til the moon and the sun were____ float - in' side by side.____ He looked in the mir - ror and his eyes____ were clear for____ the first time____ in a while,____ in____ a while. Oh,____

Verse 2:
For one split second, she almost turned around,
But that would be like pouring raindrops back into a cloud.
So, she took another step and said,
"I see the way out and I'm gonna take it."
(To Chorus:)

Verse 3:
Another glass of whiskey, but it still don't kill the pain.
He stumbles to the sink and pours it down the drain.
He said, "It's time to be a man and stop living for yesterday;
Gotta face it."
(To Chorus:)

WATCHING YOU

Words and Music by
RODNEY ATKINS, STEVE DEAN
and BRIAN WHITE

Chorus 1 & 2:

1. He said, "I've been watching you, Dad, ain't that cool? I'm your buck-a-roo; I want to
2. *See additional lyrics*

be like you. And eat all my food and grow as tall as you are.

We got cow-boy boots and cam-o pants. Yeah, we're just a-like, hey, ain't

we, Dad? I want to do ev-'ry-thing you do;

Chorus 3:

Verse 2:
We got back home and I went to the barn.
I bowed my head and I prayed real hard,
Said, "Lord, please help me help my stupid self."
Just this side of bedtime later that night,
Turnin' on my son's Scooby-Doo night-light.
He crawled out of bed and he got down on his knees.
He closed his little eyes, folded his little hands,
Spoke to God like he was talkin' to a friend.
And I said, "Son, now where'd you learn to pray like that?"
(To Chorus 2:)

Chorus 2:
He said, "I've been watching you, Dad, ain't that cool?
I'm your buckaroo; I want to be like you.
And eat all my food and grow as tall as you are.
We like fixin' things and holding Mama's hand,
Yeah, we're just alike, hey, ain't we, Dad?
I want to do everything you do; so I've been watching you."
(To Bridge:)

WAY BACK TEXAS

Gtr. tuned down 1/2 step:

⑥ = E♭　③ = G♭
⑤ = A♭　② = B♭
④ = D♭　① = E♭

Words and Music by
WENDELL MOBLEY and CRAIG WISEMAN

Moderately fast country rock (♩ = 138)

1. Some-times it's a car,____
2. *See additional lyrics*

____ a cer-tain shade_ of mys-tic blue,____ I

Way Back Texas - 7 - 1

Chorus:

back Tex - as, where you're lay - in' in___ my___ arms;___ ___ had a class - ring neck - lace. We're gon - na buy that lit - tle farm___ way down___ by the riv - er, yeah,___ raise a fam - i - ly,___

Verse 2:
Me, I'm doing well,
No one in particular.
Girl, I heard that you went and rang them weddin' bells.
They say his name is John,
His daddy owns a dealership.
But the slipper don't quite fit.
Yet life goes on and on.
(To Pre-chorus 2:)

WHENEVER YOU REMEMBER

Words and Music by
DIANE WARREN

Mm.

Verse:

1. When you look back on times we
2. When you think back on all we've

had, I hope you smile
done, I hope you're proud,

and know that thru' the good and
When you look back and see how

A WOMAN'S LOVE

Words and Music by
ALAN JACKSON

A Woman's Love - 5 - 1

YOU NEVER TAKE ME DANCING

Gtr. tuned down 1 whole step:
⑥ = D   ③ = F
⑤ = G   ② = A
④ = C   ① = D

Words and Music by
RICHARD MARX

Moderately slow blues rock (♩ = 84)

You Never Take Me Dancing - 8 - 1

Some guys___ are Ro - me - os,

oth - ers sim - ply do___ the best___ they can.___

F#7
E7

A7
G7

I'm just your av - er - age___ or - di - nar - y Joe,___

F#7
E7

B7
A7

try'n' to learn___ the things___ I nev - er knew I had___ to know.___

cresc.

Chorus:

Final Chorus:

Verse 3:
Think I do a lot to show
How I feel about her in my way.
Roses on our anniversary,
Candlelight and me on her birthday.
Just when I thought that I
Had it all worked out,
She says I still don't know
Just what it's all about.
(To Chorus:)